No Excuses!

A Brief Survival Guide to Freshman Composition

D1413999

No Excuses!

A Brief Survival Guide to Freshman Composition

Carolina Hospital

Sonoran Desert Books
Miami

SONORAN DESERT BOOKS
Miami, Florida

No Excuses! A Brief Survival Guide to Freshman Composition
Copyright © 2014 by Carolina Hospital

First Sonoran Desert Books Edition: January 2014

CONTENTS

V

Introduction
It's Not What You're Used To

A laborer works with his hands.
A craftsman works with his hands and his mind.
An artist works with his hands, his mind, and his heart.

As a teen in Queens, New York, my husband spent most afternoons at his best friend Tony's two story brick stone house. Tony's mom, Carmen, welcomed them with loud hugs and tasty Puerto Rican dishes, while Tony's father, Ed, an Italian subway supervisor, quietly worked in his basement building intricate bookshelves, tables, and dressers. His hobby, carpentry, had become his vocation. Years later, when Tony died, much too young, in a car accident, Ed gave my husband a wooden tablet which hangs over our writing desk. The inscription reads: "A laborer works with his hands. A craftsman works with his hands and his mind. An artist works with his hands, his mind, and his heart."

It doesn't matter if you want to be a carpenter, or a nurse, an accountant, a physical therapist or even a writer in a required freshman composition class, to succeed you must be willing to sweat (physically and mentally), to learn and practice your craft, and to share of yourself - your ideas, your experiences, your beliefs, even at times, your hurts. In other words, you will need to use your hands, your mind, and your heart.

Your attitude towards an activity greatly determines its outcome, as well as its gratification. When pressed, beginning writers often admit why they failed at a writing assignment: "I didn't do much;" "I was rushing;" "I didn't revise enough;" "I couldn't get into it;" "I kept changing topics." In other words, they didn't commit themselves to the process. *No Excuses!* This little book will motivate and steer you to become a terrific writer. If taken earnestly, it will offer you much more than a good grade, though that would be sweet too.

****

A writing class can be intimidating, yet most of the principles that shape the writing process parallel those in our everyday lives.

Do you cook? Talk on the cell phone? Play tennis? Run?

If so, then you are familiar with writing. Like most pursuits, these activities demand many of the elements necessary for successful writing: pattern, organization, coherence, unity, discipline, consistency... Everything I'm going to tell you about writing is already inside of you; I'm just helping you to unearth it.

Have you ever wondered why your mom yells out, "You're just like your father!" in the middle of every argument?

Or why butterflies are attracted to bright flowers?

Or why a car wastes more gas when its tires are deflated?

If you pondered a while, I'm sure you'd figure out the answers. In fact, all you have to do is make the connections. That's how writing works. It's about observations and associations. As you go about your day, the world reveals itself to you, so pay attention.

Writers always pay attention, even at the risk of being rude. For the next few months, consider yourself a writer. So, act like a writer! Eavesdrop, stare, snoop, spy. You have permission. Record what you see, hear, touch, taste, and feel.

Listen to an argument between partners, watch for unusual cloud formations, and note the bitter aftertaste of expired milk.

Look for relationships between events, conversations, objects; some ordinary and familiar, others curious and strange, shouting out for your attention.

Why should you trust my advice?

Last Friday, as I entered my favorite coffee shop, a familiar voice, said, "Professor Hospital?" "Yes," I answered, taking a better look at the face behind the voice. The waitress was a former student. She quickly updated me: she was finishing her

Bachelor's Degree in psychology at the university to where she had transferred. I was delighted she remembered me, but not surprised.

I often meet my students around town working at hospitals, restaurants, or offices. I also receive letters from former students finishing upper level degrees in law, literature, physics, or foreign languages.

For 25 years, I have taught college Freshman Composition; I have also published essays, poems, a novel - six books in total - but you have probably never heard of me. Fame and fortune have not visited my way. Yet I have been blessed with something more valuable: the vocation of educator. There is nothing more important and rewarding than leading students to their best work. I have taught over 9,500 college students how to communicate successfully with the written word. I hope you will become one of them.

****

A Warning

This book is not a rhetoric in the traditional sense: a formal study of the use of language with persuasive effect. Neither is it a Handbook with exhaustive information on all aspects of writing and documentation. It is even less a reader with sample essays by professionals illustrating different types of rhetorical devices. No. There are plenty of excellent books out there that do all this. I have used many throughout my extensive career as a composition teacher.

What is it then?

It is a conversation between us writers. I happen to be an author and a professor of Freshman Composition and you are a freshman writer. It is also a compilation of the best suggestions I have shared with my students to help them, not only survive, but flourish, as writers.

This book is written for you. It will empower you to succeed in and enjoy your required composition courses.

Day One
Great Expectations! –Ok, Let's Get Real…

If you stroll into your first composition course hoping you will not have to read or write much, you are in for a rude awakening. That's like signing up for a driving class and wishing you never had to touch the wheel. Of course you will have to read and write - a lot. That's the ONLY way to improve your skills! You might as well face it. A writer needs to write all the time, ideally every day, or as often as possible, at least for as long as you attend a writing class.

So, from day one, walk into your composition class with realistic expectations. You can't just *study* how to write; you must *do* it!

Most of us learn about writing in a classroom. Yet, if you think about it, most classroom courses, like history, sociology, political science, or astronomy, concentrate on content; learning to write takes skill. You don't just analyze it, you practice it. That's the goal and the challenge.

Today, as I was reviewing blank books, I came across one student who complained for two pages about how journaling was a waste of time. The student obviously missed the point, yet ironically still practiced for two pages! Writing regularly is the equivalent of rehearsing before a performance. Would you attend a piano recital without practicing ahead of time?

To put it another way, think about writing like you would about getting into shape. You go to the gym, plan a workout routine, hit the machines and stick to it. In a little while, you start seeing results: you look good and you feel good. It's the same with writing class.

Like for the gym, you will need to set a routine for writing in your daily schedule. Choose a time when you know you are free and can stick to it, whether it's 20 minutes or two hours a day, on the bus or before bed. Think of it as lab time for the class. Whether you have an assignment due the next day or the next week, you have to do the lab work!

Some days, many days, you will not feel like writing. Temptations will lure you away from your laptop: a sunny sky, a friend's evite, a much needed nap, a hungry stomach, an upcoming test, a final chapter in a mystery thriller. That's why you plan ahead. When you are not motivated, you must be disciplined. That's how the scheduling helps. The discipline propels you through the difficult times. It's easy to write when you're rested, in a good mood, and passionate about your subject matter. But what about when you're exhausted from studying for an exam, upset after a fight with a friend, or disappointed because you hate the topic the instructor has assigned? That's when discipline becomes your ally.

Of course, you must buy into the idea that the more you write, the more you'll improve. After all, isn't that why you push yourself to keep lifting weights long after it has stopped being fun and every muscle is begging you to stop? You continue to exercise because it's what you must do to improve; however, if you're practicing bad habits, practice does not always make perfect. You need to combine the discipline of regular practice with new knowledge of your craft. That's why you're taking a writing class.

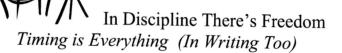

In Discipline There's Freedom
Timing is Everything (In Writing Too)

I started college undecided about my major, but convinced I would become a famous author. As an avid reader and writer since childhood, I was arrogant about my skills and determined to create a book like no other. Something never seen before or after! No one could stop me, restrain me, stifle me. I was going to be an artist and my medium would be language. I was fearless about my determination, but not about my discipline.

In my eagerness to be innovative and exceptional, I forgot that pride comes before the fall. I experienced many literary setbacks and read many rejections slips before I understood what the Catalan cellist Pablo Casals meant by "In discipline, there's freedom."

Many years have passed since I published my first poem. Since then I have published six books. I love to write and once I'm sitting down half way through a new page, I don't want to stop; however, getting me to put everything aside to start is quite a challenge. Why? The truth: it's exhausting work. Don't let anyone fool you. Thought provoking, moving, stimulating writing is grueling demanding work. It's so much easier to email a friend, shop on line, watch a movie.

Other times, I have trouble sitting down to write because I'm discouraged with my writing, angry at the publishers, frustrated by the human condition, or just too anxious to settle down. Those days, writing seems useless, especially because it takes so long to see the results. On days like these, when I feel lazy or disheartened, I rely on... my schedule.

At the beginning of every semester, I plan out my days and choose an hour, if I'm lucky two, for writing. Not for grading, answering emails or doing chores. Just for writing. When the clock strikes three o'clock for example (the designated time), I drop whatever I'm doing and sit down to write, without negotiating it.

That discipline gives me freedom. I no longer struggle every day finding time to write or making excuses to explain to myself why I couldn't do it. During that time, I am free of all other responsibilities; I am free to create.

For those minutes or hours set aside, I am fully present and focused on what I am doing. The more consistently I work on a given project - a poem, an essay, a novel, this book - the more I master my skills, and the more confident I feel about my own growth as a writer. You will too.

Be real. Choose a time when you know for sure you can be quiet, alone, without interruptions. If you have to leave your house to find that, do it. Go to a library, a bookstore, a coffee shop, a park, anywhere you can concentrate. The key is to plan for it. Block off that time slot, as if you had a class or a job, and don't deviate from it. That's the discipline. Don't second guess yourself. Don't fall to temptations. Work your writing muscles regularly.

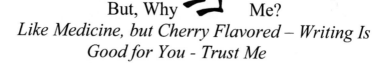

But, Why Me?
Like Medicine, but Cherry Flavored – Writing Is Good for You - Trust Me

You are probably taking a writing class as a requirement, so you might be asking yourself, why me?!

I'm never going to be a writer. I just want to own a business, teach kindergarteners, design houses, become a nurse. Why do I have to learn how to write an essay anyway?

A good question. The answer is not simple.

First, there are practical reasons. You will need to write many essays along the way to graduation. For instance, in other classes, professors will require analytical or research essays. In addition, many of your exams will include essay questions; moreover, if you transfer to another institution, it will likely ask you for an essay about yourself.

Outside of school, you will also need these skills. Some employers today even require a writing component in their interview process. Once hired, on a daily basis, you will be writing emails, reports, proposals, minutes of meetings...in each case, your writing will speak for you.

You are investing time, effort, sweat, and money into your education. Don't you want to sound like you've done so? When someone is reading your words, they are hearing you without seeing you. Your written words should reflect the best of your education.

Other benefits are not immediately obvious; however, as you hone your skills, sharpen your tools, and stretch beyond your comfort level to enhance your writing, you will automatically grow in other domains as well. A strong essay will be focused, organized, creative, insightful, and clear. As you progress in each of these areas, you will also improve as a verbal communicator, a thinker, even a leader. Mastering the craft of writing imparts enormous confidence. By learning to control ideas and words, you will feel empowered by your ability to conquer language.

Finally, if you work diligently to acquire these skills and learn to discipline yourself, you will turn a simple writing assignment into a work of art. You will transform mediocrity into excellence. That in itself provides immense gratification.

Take for example how David felt after one of my assignments. I shared with his classmates his essay on Seminole Indian Leader Osceola, a lucid and moving piece of writing. As I read it aloud, David, who usually sat quietly, yet attentively, in the back of the room, beamed with pride. People got what he meant. That satisfaction is the best reward of a well written piece.

The gains of writing reach way beyond effective articulation and word usage. Effective writing bestows confidence and exhilaration. Through writing, you can make limitless discoveries about yourself and your capabilities, as no doubt others will make about you.

Forget About Easy
The Pain/Pleasure Principle: Getting Your Heart and Your Brain on Paper

Learning to write well brings many rewards, but it does take rigor. As I approached one of my students yesterday, I detected apprehension. I asked her to show me the changes to her essay we had discussed earlier; she hesitated and said, "I don't get it. It's so hard."

"Yes it is," I replied. "So?"

Writing is hard work. It will ask much from you. You will need to be creative and analytical, patient and quick-thinking, restrained and vulnerable. But then, the most valuable things in life do not come easily, right?

It takes persistence and compromise to solidify a relationship. It takes determination and resilience to succeed as an athlete. It takes discipline and technique to master an instrument.

The best things in life do not come in an App. We cannot Google them for a quick answer or TiVo them for a rainy day. We need to sweat for them.

Writing is no different. Creating a memorable essay means exertion. It means mental sweat. It is not an accident. It takes, first of all, knowledge of the craft. As a writer, you must acquire the techniques necessary to be effective. You can obtain these by reading books like this one, taking a composition class, talking to other writers, visiting a writing center, and absorbing great works of literature. Then, most importantly, you must apply these tools.

Perseverance, discipline and resourcefulness are indispensable traits for all worthwhile goals, including writing. There's no way around it; to improve, you need to practice.

Yes, the rewards of writing are countless, but only if you succeed. An uninspired, mundane, general piece of writing comes effortlessly, but brings no satisfaction to the reader or the writer. The little devil on your shoulder may tempt you to take the quick way out of every assignment. *Choose a broad topic - easier. Pick the familiar subject - easier. Take on the simpler perspective - easier.* True, a broad, familiar, simple topic will be

18

undemanding, but not more effective. In fact, easier often leads to boring and boring is the enemy of both the reader and the writer!

A vivid, moving, and poignant piece of writing will fascinate the reader and will fill you with exhilaration, delight and pride. Nevertheless, every stage of the process will demand time and effort, from narrowing the topics, to finding good details and examples; from organizing effectively, to revising the language, over and over again. So roll up your sleeves and let's get to work.

The Language of Writing is Reading
Reading your Way toward Writer's Nirvana

One of my former students, Nick, came by the office to-day to pick up his portfolio. On his way out, he remarked: "Why didn't you warn me about *The Grapes of Wrath*?"

I had no idea what he meant.

"It's so sad," he added.

"What did you expect Nick? It's a novel about the depression, migrant workers, the Dust Bowl?"

"I know, but I thought maybe…"

We continued talking about Steinbeck's book until I asked him if he had read other novels during the summer.

"Sure, I haven't stopped reading since class ended."

His words tasted like chocolate to me and I love chocolate.

Get ready. Most writing teachers will require you to read. Reading is the language of writing – not conversations, text messages, or movies. Ask any professional writer for advice on how to improve your writing. Nine out of ten times, the first response will be: "Read! Read, read, read, as much as you can."

When you read, you are immersed in a sea of words; that alone helps. In addition, reading stimulates your mind and your senses; provides you with content and context; teaches you vocabulary usage; but most of all, exposes you to the rhythms and intonations of the written language.

Have you noticed how easily you recognize the voices of friends and relatives over the phone? Likewise, every writer has a unique voice with a distinct rhythm. The rhythm of an essay is achieved through sentence structure, punctuation, figurative language, vocabulary, diction, sentence length – everything. By reading, you absorb those skills without even trying. The more you read, the more familiar you become with the art of writing.

If you increase your reading, your essays will improve, in spite of yourself.

Choose your reading material carefully as you develop this habit. First, select a book that interests you. Dare to try new things; you would be surprised. If you've read every book by Anne Rice, then try Ray Bradbury. It's not that her books aren't helpful and fun. It's just that you want to expose yourself to different rhythms and styles, vocabulary and diction.

Don't forget to consider the level of difficulty. If the book is too simple for your level, your skills will not grow. On the other hand, if a book is beyond your abilities at the moment, you will probably feel frustrated and quit. That defeats the purpose. Take your time choosing. I could give you a list of my favorite books, but that's not the point. You need to discover your own. To help you start, I will include at the end some choices my students repeatedly enjoy. I purposely keep a varied list.

You can also ask your teacher for suggestions or talk to your friends about what they are reading or have recently read. Go to the local bookstore or library and browse around the fiction aisles. Pick up a book, read the jacket, perhaps even the first few pages. Try different types of books.

Once you decide on one, give it time. A book is like a relationship. You can't talk to someone for five minutes and dismiss him or her. You need to give people time to really get to know them. Sometimes, people surprise you, don't they?

The same happens with books. As much as I love to read, I admit, I'm a slow starter. It takes me easily 30-50 pages before I'm truly engaged by a book. Then, I can't put the darn thing down until I finish! Don't give up too easily. Read a while. Most books, like people, ultimately grab hold.

Some of my students confess they have never read a novel cover to cover, so the idea can be scary. If that's your case, more reason to choose your book wisely. There is a novel out there waiting for you. Keep searching and choose for yourself. Just because your brother, girlfriend, mother or teacher liked it, doesn't mean you will. There are great novels and memoirs that revolve around sports, cars, war, fishing, nature, espionage, crime, gangs, fantasy, and of course romance. Find one that you can enjoy. Reading should not be a punishment, but a pleasure. Of course, like any new habit, at first, it takes some effort and patience, so don't give up.

There's More to Writing than Writing

Trekking

In addition to reading, daily life offers invaluable material for writing. Before looking at the process itself of writing an essay, or its structure, let's think about the content. What the heck do you write about? How do you find something interesting to say?

Frank McCourt, the author of *Angela's Ashes*, once said about life: "Nothing is significant, until you make it significant." Some people sit around waiting for something significant to happen. Life doesn't work that way. You need to make it happen. The same applies to writing. Only you can uncover what is noteworthy or relevant in your life.

McCourt, for example, grew up in Ireland, the son of a frequently unemployed alcoholic, who drank up what little he earned until he abandoned the family. After surviving a childhood and adolescence of poverty and deprivation, McCourt immigrated to the United States and eventually taught 27 years in the New York public high school system.

Only after retiring at 68, did he complete his memoir *Angela's Ashes* which, published in 27 countries and translated into 17 languages, sold over four million copies.

This humble retired teacher turned a life of adversity into something significant, entertaining, and inspiring for millions of people. That's what writing can accomplish. Each of us has a story worth telling. Let me say that again: each of us has a story worth telling. Believe in yourself and your ideas. Observe your own life with dignity; explore it with curiosity and face it, in spite of any fears.

When you write, have something to say. If you're asked to write about yourself, look at your life from the outside in. Reflect on the events, people, cultural customs and beliefs that have shaped you. Look at family photographs; find a family tree. Probe relatives for stories of your youth, their youth. Recollect moments that make you flush with anger, embarrassment, or shame. You do have a tale to tell. Dig until you find it.

If you are assigned an expository topic, open your mind to ideas and perspectives beyond your experiences or even interests. Find connections and make them relatable to your reader.

To help you accomplish this, read about everything: history, art, war, physics, fishing. The more you learn about something, the more you'll be interested in it. The deeper you travel into a subject, the more you'll want to continue exploring it, for yourself, as well as your reader.

In addition, plunge into unfamiliar activities: learn a new sport, new instrument, or new language; visit a book fair or museum; attend a play; go canoeing or bird watching; bike in a nearby state park; visit a historical site. In other words, find stimulation. Stretch. These activities will seem irrelevant to your writing topic, but they are not. They will help you to make new associations and come up with inventive angles.

Writing is an extension of you, so how you embrace or reject your own story or the world around you is integral to your success. You make the choice. Be bored and thus boring, or stimulated and thus stimulating.

In Process We Trust
The Three Commandments:
Preparation/Drafting/Rewriting

I
First Commandment: Preparation

Would it make sense to chop an onion after dropping it into the spaghetti sauce, or to shorten the legs of a chair after just painting it? What a mess!

From photosynthesis, to childbirth, to construction, most things follow a process: a series of actions or events directed towards a goal that produces a similar outcome each time. Writing is no exception.

Understanding this, that writing demands process, will help you approach it more effectively. Each stage must be fulfilled in order to reach your destination - a strong essay - successfully. For the sake of simplification, we can call these stages preparation, drafting and rewriting.

First, ask yourself. Once the teacher assigns a topic, do you usually hurry to start your rough draft? You are not alone. Unfortunately, most beginning writers rush to write too soon.

Be patient. Generate ideas; then, organize them.

How do you generate ideas?

Given a choice, write about what you know well: your family, your city, your favorite sport, your passions, your frustrations. If you're assigned a subject matter, you still need ideas to help you focus. Let's say your instructor chooses the broad topic: "Your Culture." Begin by narrowing down the different elements of culture; then choose one you relate to most: food, music, language, religion, sports?

Don't hurry. You will not save time. Instead you will set yourself up for a sluggish, frustrating experience.

Relax. Becoming anxious about the assignment will only thwart the creative juices. Linger with your subject and allow the writing to loosen up your ideas.

Experienced writers use different methods to help them. Before drafting your essay, or even outlining it, try one or more of these exercises:

1) Write at the top of a page your topic, then, jot down all the words or phrases that pop in your brain without judging them. (Brainstorming)

2) Choose a length of time, perhaps 20 minutes, and write down whatever ideas buzz around in your head, but this time in sentences, like you were composing a letter or a diary entry. It may look like an essay when you are done, but don't be fooled. It's not, yet. (Free writing)

3) Place your topic in the middle of the page, then bunch your ideas according to categories into circled clusters around the center topic as they elbow their way into your thoughts. (Clustering)

4) Pretend you are a reporter and find out what you would want to know about this topic. (Interviewing Yourself)

5) Talk to a friend about the topic; pick up some magazines or books; cruise the web. Jot down ideas. In short, look for stimulation outside of yourself. (Researching)

Notice, all the techniques demand some sort of writing, not just thinking! Thinking alone is not good enough. Just today, I asked a student sitting in front of a blank page why she had not brought her rough draft. "I couldn't think about anything that has changed in my life," she said.

She had not begun to write a thing down, in spite of the fact that her adolescence had been abruptly uprooted at 14 when she moved with her mom to Miami from Philadelphia. She also mentioned later how her aunt's personality had transformed negatively after being diagnosed with breast cancer at 44. When I asked the student why she didn't choose to explore one of those two topics, she answered, "I didn't think I had enough to write about in each case." Of course not, she hadn't used any of the above exercises to generate ideas.

Her problem was not lack of information, but lack of technique and effort. Either topic would make a wonderful essay, but her "thinking about it," was obviously not enough to produce results.

As we think, we forget at least half of what drops in on our consciousness. Moreover, as ideas emerge, we judge them too harshly. We discard them because we find them too boring, too ordinary, too difficult. This happens less when actually writing. The mind is too busy holding the pen or striking the keyboard to scrutinize every thought.

Give these methods a try. They work. Let the writing guide you and be open to surprises.

If you've tried some of these exercises and you're still struggling with your ideas, take a nap, go for a walk, swim a while. Stressing out is not the solution. Creativity flows more easily when you are relaxed. Let it come to you; don't force it. You cannot catch a ball if you clench your hands.

Legend says that Thomas Edison would sit in an arm chair holding a ball bearing. He would rotate it in the palm of his hand until he became drowsy. If he fell asleep, his hand would drop and the sound of the ball bearing hitting the ground would wake him. He'd then start the activity all over again. His goal was not to fall asleep, but to find himself in a tranquil state that stimulated his theories.

Assuming you've had success gathering a bunch of ideas and details, you're ready for the next step in your preparations: making choices.

You must discard some details, maybe many. How do you decide? Find a focus, a main idea to control the entire essay. Like when choosing a college major, once that's done, selecting classes suddenly becomes a cinch.

The sentence that articulates that main idea is called by writers, the thesis. (Suggestions on developing an effective thesis will be discussed in a later chapter.) Once you settle on your focus, then you can prioritize the rest of your points, examples, and details.

To organize these, develop an outline. It's a way of deciding what you are including and excluding, and in which order you will place it. Outlining helps to maintain unity and control over your essay. Keep in mind that it is not written in stone; it is a work in progress, like your essay. As you write and re-write, you may need to revisit and adjust your outline. That's fine. Its purpose is to give you a skeleton on which to expand, not stifle you.

Start your informal outline by writing down your thesis. Even if you aren't sure, choose something, so you can keep going. The writing process will help you confirm whether or not you've selected wisely. Then, make up your mind which key points best illustrate or develop the main idea. Number them. Most people aim for three, but two or four may work just as well, depending on your topic and the length of your essay. Once you've written down these points, then look for a few details and/or examples for each and write them under the appropriate main point. Voila! An outline.

Some students like to write multiple free writing drafts instead of outlining. That can work as long as you are aware when you are shifting into a more formal draft. In other words, each draft reduces a bit more the focus and plays with perspectives until you arrive at a clear focal point with a definitive path.

Whether free writing or outlining, remember, don't rush. Linger with your topic. Wait until you have enough to say before moving forward.

Just this week a student came to my office to discuss an unsuccessful essay. The first words out of his mouth were "I'm not a creative writer!" I quickly pointed out that his essay had included a weak thesis which lead to a disorganized mess of ideas. When I asked him if he had developed an outline, even a quick one - a thesis with three major points – he shook his head. Bingo. Lack of planning was his problem, not lack of creativity.

General judgments, such as "I lack creativity" or "I'm a bad writer" or "I had bad teachers" or "I hated my English classes," only serve as a crutch to avoid sweating the work now. Look forward.

Second Commandment: Drafting

Ready for your rough draft?

The drafting stage should be a creative sprint of energy. That can only happen after planning. If you start too soon, you will obstruct the creative process. You want the second stage to be a discovery. Again, trust the process; it will open you up to unexpected ideas and insights.

You might have been tempted to start writing as soon as you were assigned your topic. Bad idea. It will not save time because you will need to stop along the way to think. If that happens, and the progress is slow-moving, you will also become exasperated and discouraged. Imagine participating in a marathon without training? You will not run a successful race, plus you will likely get injured and avoid running for a long time. So if you have not prepared, stop now and do so.

Maybe you didn't rush in to start writing, but you are anxious to rush out. To achieve that, you may be tempted to proofread each sentence and even each paragraph as you draft. Again, a lousy idea. Because drafting is an inventive stage, you do not want to "clean as you go." That's only good in the kitchen.

You don't want to invest too much time and energy in your initial draft. Why? What if you discover, at the end of your rough draft, that you want to eliminate half the essay? Or shift focus? Or change the examples? That's great! But if you have spent time cleaning up each sentence, you will not want to touch a thing; in fact, you may refuse to do so, because you will be too invested and too attached!

The same happens in relationships, no? Some people feel too invested, too attached or too loyal to a partner to break up even when problems rear their ugly head. That is why it's important to choose wisely and give the relationship time.

If you are looking to buy a car and want a great deal, a good suggestion is not to get fixated on any one vehicle. The salesman will spot you a mile away. Walk in willing to walk out. Otherwise, you will fail in your mission.

An essay is neither a partner nor a car, but the principle is the same. Do not invest too much energy on any one sentence, until you are sure, it's going to stay.

Moreover, stopping to clean up a sentence as you write will interrupt the creative flow. Avoid that. Let the ideas burst out; relax and enjoy. There will be time to worry later.

III
The Third Commandment: Rewrite

"Professor, I'm such a bad writer. I don't know what to do?" A student confessed once.

"I don't see it that way," I answered. "You have strong writing skills and your essays have been interesting."

"But if you only knew," she replied.

"Knew what?" I joked with her. "Your mother wrote the papers?"

"No!" she said. "If you only knew how many times I have to revise my essays before they work."

Many beginning writers feel this way. They think a good writer should create a perfect essay in one draft. IMPOSSIBLE! No one can do that. Revision is part of the writing. In fact, the better the writer, the more drafts, because the expectations rise.

Think about it. Musicians practice more, not less, as their skills improve and the compositions become more challenging. The same happens with all activities requiring skills, including writing.

After your initial draft comes the real work of writing. The third stage should make you sweat. If your rough draft looks like your final draft, you've failed, so don't rush ahead to fix your spelling and punctuation. You're far from that point. Before you begin to worry about the mechanics of the writing, worry about the substance.

Most beginning writers hate this stage – I used to – because it's the most demanding. But you'll grow to like it, if you see it as one last challenge on the way toward a great essay. So,

30

once you have a finished draft, ask yourself numerous questions:

Is this what I wanted to say? Did I present it in a clear and interesting way? Will anyone want to read it other than me? Do I have unity of focus? Do I have enough details? Examples? Transitions? Figurative language? Does my introduction draw in the reader? Does my conclusion end with a bang?

If you answered NO to ANY of these questions, then you are ready for revision, the most important phase, when the text transforms from an average uninspired assignment to a powerful effective essay. To accomplish this, you must be willing to mutilate, dissect, alter, rearrange, even reconstruct your first draft. This process demands a big chunk of your time.

Expect to make multiple revisions. Every aspect of the writing cannot be evaluated all at once. You need to read the essay multiple times, looking at different elements each time.

If you're satisfied with the content of your essay, you can begin to look at the way you have expressed those ideas and examples. Evaluate your language for wordiness and improve your sentence structures. Be more concise and add variety and emphasis. In other words, make sure you have communicated in a clear, direct, and interesting way to your reader. Later chapters will provide specific examples to help you improve in these areas.

Only then, when you are satisfied with the content and the language, will you be ready for the last step: editing the mechanics by looking for grammar, punctuation, and spelling errors.

Extensive rewriting is the key to composing effective essays. Understanding the overall process makes a huge difference. Use it to your advantage.

Oh, yes! Don't forget to read your essay out loud! At the expense of sounding crazy to your relatives or roommates, read every word out loud. It will help you make final improvements. If something doesn't make sense, you will hear it. Of course, this may mean making even more changes. Yes. Writing is fluid. Be willing to move with the flow. It will make your writing more successful and even more fun.

The Body Essay
From Head to Toe: It's the Structure, Stupid

I
Introduction

An essay is not a machine. It's a reflection and expression of a human being's ideas, observations, attitudes, moods.

If you understand how the human body works, then you understand how an essay works, as something live, vibrant and fluid, not mechanical, formulaic or robotic.

The different sections of an essay function similarly to those of a person. A typical essay contains three parts: an introduction, a body, and a conclusion. These are **not** the equivalent of paragraphs, but rather components. You can write a 4, 5, 7, or 25 paragraph essay and it will still include these same three elements.

In fact, most communication functions similarly. Take the simplest cell phone conversation:

"Hey, it's me. How're you doing?"

"Great. What's up?"

"Busy tonight?"

(Introduction)

"No, why?"

"I'm thinking of the movies. Want to come?"

"Sure, what time?"

"Eight, I'll pick you up at 7:30."

(Body)

"Fine, text me when you're on the way."

"Will do. Bye."

(Conclusion)

The introduction acts like the human head, with its expressive eyes and controlling brain. Like a stranger's eyes, which can draw you in or repel you, the first sentence or two of your essay should capture the reader's attention. **Hook** your reader early by writing something original, unpredictable, clever, moving, or controversial. There's no point in spending end-

32

less hours developing your ideas in the body if the reader gives up after the first few lines. So make sure to always revise your hook. Try different techniques: a vivid description, a thought provoking quote that relates to your topic, a shocking statistic, a series of examples, a human interest story (an anecdote). Writers often combine these; they also play with the words themselves to draw you in.

Don't be afraid to take risks with the language. For example, what if I said, "Last month, I went to Atlanta." You probably wouldn't care much. What if instead I said, "Last month, I had to go to Atlanta." You'd probably want to know, why? No? You're hooked. That's what you want for your readers, to capture them so they will continue reading. The change in only one word, in this case the verb, can make all the difference.

Be careful however not to overdo the hook. It should not attract attention to itself, but cunningly draw in the reader to the rest of your essay.

Tip: Never let the hook hold you back from starting the essay. Remarkable ones don't come quickly. Draft your essay even if you realize your first few lines need further attention. Develop your points and later revise. You will discover your hook in the process. Not uncommonly, as I review student essays, I will point out an original phrase, a moving recollection, or a compelling example in the body of the text which could make a perfect start. So don't fret over the hook until much later.

The thesis, on the other hand, must be developed early because it works like the brain of this "human" essay.

Before including the thesis, however, incorporate some background information on the general subject of the essay. If the topic involves a problem, this is a good time to bring it up. If you are analyzing literature, you may want to briefly introduce the author of the work or review its historical context. In other words, provide the reader a path towards your main point, but do not write more than you need. Don't use the introduction to warm up because you run the risk of including two introductions. Also beware not to give away too much in the introduction or you'll lose the reader's interest later. It's like giving up the punch line too soon. Find the perfect balance. Make sure what you have included is just enough to get the reader headed in the right direction. The topic, not you, should dictate the length of the introduction.

In one of my class assignments, I asked the students to choose a Florida city and a 50 year time period to explore how geography and environment impacted its development during that time. One student, who chose St. Augustine, used the introduction to give a brief historical overview of the town from early Spanish colonial rule until the 19th century. As she developed the introduction, she began to narrow her focus until she arrived at her destination for the entire essay: "Because of St. Augustine's tropical weather and coastal location, Henry Flagler saw an opportunity for development and tourism that would modernize America's oldest city." That destination is **the thesis** statement.

Most writers include the thesis at the end of the introduction, but that's not necessarily the end of the first paragraph. Remember, the introduction is a component of the essay, not simply the first paragraph. It may take you two paragraphs, even three, to introduce your topic, depending on the overall length and complexity of your essay. That's fine. When you are finished with the background, that's when you insert the thesis.

The thesis sentence articulates the main idea of the entire essay. Its function is twofold: to narrow the scope of the topic and to offer a distinct viewpoint on it. That is, the angle from which you will be looking at your main idea. In the case of the previous topic, the focus is the specific city during the 19th century and the viewpoint is how geography and climate favorably encouraged that city's development.

Three students could be focusing on the same topic, let's say, coral reefs; however, each one could approach this subject from a unique perspective. One student could concentrate on the plant and animal diversity in the reefs. Another could explore how they are the most threatened marine life in the globe. Finally, a third writer could discuss efforts at managing and preserving reefs in the Florida Keys. Some overlapping could emerge, yet each student could pursue his or her own perspective on the shared focus: the reefs.

To put it another way, if you are writing an essay on how a particular event in your youth marked you, then the specific event, like the death of your cousin, would be your focus. The life altering impact his death left on your personal attitudes would be your viewpoint. Your thesis might read: *When my cousin, a victim of gang violence, was shot down,* (focus) *I re-evaluated my own views on aggression and drugs* (viewpoint).

From time to time, a student will say "I know what I want to write about, but I can't write it down." I don't believe it. If you can't write it down, it's usually because you're still not sure about your focus. Do the work. Keep generating ideas until you can develop a confident thesis statement. Decide on your destination before you plan out the directions. It'll make for a smoother journey by allowing you to determine early which points, ideas, details, examples, or comparisons will best support the direction and tone of your essay.

If your essay caught fire, you'd want to grab your thesis and run. That's how important it is. With it, you can begin to develop your points.

One last word on the location of the thesis. Some teachers may have suggested you place it at the opening of your essay. This works for beginning writers to help them control the text from the onset. Nevertheless, as you read more, and mature as a writer, you will find that most advanced authors prefer to lead with a hook, provide background, and then end the introduction with the thesis. It is too important a sentence to risk at the beginning of the essay where the reader might overlook it. That's why it's best to save it for the end of the introduction. In addition, placing it at the end allows you to draw in the reader first; then, easily jump from the thesis, at the end of the intro, into the body of the essay.

II
The Torso

If the introduction with its thesis is the brain of the essay, then the body is its torso. And like a torso, it supports the thesis. It is composed of a series of paragraphs that describe, develop, explain, illustrate, and/or defend the thesis statement. It's the most analytical section of the essay, requiring clear organization and control over the focus. Each paragraph must relate back to the thesis in some way.

If you have outlined your ideas, you're ready to continue drafting. If not, go back to the drawing board and make sure you have enough points to discuss; then, arrange them down in the most logical order. Differentiate between major and minor points, as well as the details and examples that will illustrate these. Ask yourself, should I organize these spatially, from top to bottom and right to left, or chronologically, from infancy to adulthood, or from morning to night? Or should I organize these in order of importance, or from general to specific? Find a reasonable way to present your materials to the reader.

A typical body paragraph consists of 5 to 8 sentences; however, you should not determine where to start a new paragraph simply by counting lines. Every paragraph contains its own focus. In fact, body paragraphs can be called mini-essays. They begin (or end sometimes) with a **topic sentence** that directs the content, followed by a combination of details, examples, ideas, comparisons, statistics, facts, quotes. Note how this list includes neither broad generalities nor repetitive observations. You want muscle, not flab, in those body paragraphs. If you do not have enough concrete information, then brainstorm or research more.

After you have developed your point enough, end your paragraph with something that gives it a sense of closure. Don't just leave it hanging with one last statistic or example. Let the reader know you are winding down and getting ready to switch.

If you find your body paragraph stretching too long, then find a natural way of dividing it. In an essay about your parents' influence on you, for instance, you might want to separate the section on genetic pre-determination into several paragraphs, each discussing a different area where genetics has played a key role in your development.

Between paragraphs, make sure to **transition** from one idea or point or example to another. Establish the links for the readers. They shouldn't have to guess the relationships between your paragraphs.

In fact, always connect your ideas, not just between paragraphs, but also between sentences. Some people refer to these as sentence connectors. Beware of using the lazy "and" as your main sentence connector, it reveals little if anything about the relationship between ideas.

Writing, like all effective communication, is about making connections. As a writer, it's your role to make these for the reader.

III

The Conclusion

Let's say you are invited to a party where you're sure to run into your ex. You get a haircut and buy a new outfit. When it's time to get dressed, you realize you forgot matching shoes.

If you wear the perfect shoes, people might not notice them, but instead rave about your overall appearance; however, if you wear a pair of tacky shoes, they will surely take note, hardly perceiving the rest of your brilliant attire. That's life and that's how it works in writing as well.

Don't underestimate the importance of the conclusion. It provides the last taste of your essay. Make sure it enhances the rest of the essay, not detract from its general flavor. In your revision process, tinker with the sentences until you create an interesting compelling end. A summary or re-statement of your thesis is not forceful enough.

As you read, pay attention to how essays or articles end. Some writers conclude with a reflective look back, making some inferences about the ideas discussed. Others use a thought-provoking quote or an anecdote. Analogies are commonly used as well. Finally, writers will offer alternatives and suggestions or make calls to action, especially in argumentative essays. Try one or a few of these techniques to formulate a powerful conclusion. It will give your essay that final touch of excellence.

Once you understand how the various parts of an overall essay work, you are ready to look at the language itself.

Bring Me the THING over There!
Like, What Are You Talking About?

If you ask a friend, "Bring me that thing over there," he'll most likely reply, "What thing?" You'll probably respond by repeating the exact same words, "Bring me that thing over there," only this time shouting and pointing to the object. Your friend will immediately understand what you mean: the notebook on top of the cabinet. Was it his words that revealed the answer? Hardly.

Many of us wander through life saying the equivalent of "Bring me the thing over there," without a problem; however, what is really doing the communicating? In most circumstances, it's the body language: the hand gestures, the body stance, the tone of the words, even the pitch of the voice.

The language of conversation is not the language of writing. When we speak, most of us instinctively rely on our bodies to help us communicate. Without thinking about it, our bodies provide information, sometimes even more effectively than our words. Remember the friend who hollered *she wasn't angry*? Or the classmate, who in a muffled disheartened voice, insisted *he was fine*?

We understand guardedness when we see crossed arms, or impatience when we hear nails tapping. Not a word is needed.

When you write, however, the reader cannot see you communicating with non-verbal gestures or ask you to elaborate on your confusing statement. When you write, words are your only tools, so you need to use them to show your meaning, clearly and vividly.

Sometimes beginning writers think English teachers are too picky. When a teacher writes on the border of the page, *Be more precise*, you might shrug your shoulders and ask yourself, who cares if I call a knob, a handle? After all, they both open doors. But what if the door with the handle meant your exit from a fire raging behind the door with a knob? In that case, it would make a life or death difference, no? Words do make a difference.

The words you choose, along with the way you organize and punctuate them, determine how effectively you can communicate. That is why being precise, concise, and especially vivid - the topics of the next few pages - are essential to good writing.

Make it HD!
I
Those Vivid Details

When you think about your childhood, what comes to mind?

For me, it's the pungent scent of ripe mangoes bust open on the hot sidewalks, or the sounds of my Sunday mornings: Schubert's violins accompanying my mother's clinking and pounding in the kitchen, as the aroma of her grilling onions and garlic snakes its way up to my room. I can see the hibiscus hedge with large pink and red blossoms surrounding our house and feel the sugar on my lips as I bite into the soft buns of *pan dulce*. I can hear the chirping coming from the box *papi* proudly carries into the house filled with tiny duckling fur balls.

The details of these events are branded on my mind as if they had taken place just yesterday instead of years ago. Why? They stimulate my senses: I smell the fruit, hear the notes, see the bright petals against the green; I taste the sugary delicacies and I feel the silky chick.

Like in a memory, if you want to write about something that leaves an imprint on your readers – stimulate their senses. Use triggers that will allow them to visualize your words. Find the details that will allow you to do so. Become a detective of your own experiences.

At first, you will uncover many visual details of color, size, shape, but don't stop there. Search for sounds, tastes and textures as well, even when you are describing abstract elements. For example, what does fear taste like? bitter? or maybe dry?

In Freshman Composition, most instructors start with personal essays. The advantage here is that you are familiar with the material: yourself. In writing about yourself, you will need to both tell and show. Telling, a sort of summarizing, comes easier to beginning writers. The challenge is in the showing. Coming up with the specific details that stimulate the senses is hard enough, but you also have to work on finding the precise words that depict those details. Make the Thesaurus your friend. Keep searching until you find just the word you want.

For example, if you are writing about the effects of a hurricane on your neighborhood, make sure you can identify the types of trees that lost their branches: oak? mahogany? black olive? ficus? royal poinciana? Describe the window glass and roof tile debris on the driveway. Don't forget the sound of the hammering as people removed last minute wooden shutters or fixed broken fences. Those concrete precise details will enliven your personal essay; simply saying, "the neighborhood looked a mess," will make your writing a boring blur to the reader.

If instead of a personal essay, you are assigned expository writing where the purpose is to inform or explain, you will also need to focus on details, maybe not about yourself, but about the subject matter. In that case, be willing to do the research. If you're asked to analyze crime in your city, for example, look up statistics, of course, but don't forget to find instances of recent cases or interviews with victims or city officials of the criminal justice department in the newspaper. You can use the details in the articles, as well as the testimonials, to complement your facts.

If you are analyzing literature, choose wisely your supporting quotes. They can add energy to your piece. Take advantage of the author's vivid detailed language and weave it into your essay, always identifying the source of course! For instance, in their discussions of Hemingway's novel *The Old Man and the Sea*, students often cite the line "the sea destroyed him [the old man] but did not defeat him." They realize that with its conciseness, use of alliteration, and thematic insight, Hemingway's sentence empowers their own words.

Even when writing about abstract values and ideas, find a way to stimulate the senses. For instance, one student referred to herself as a "Cradle Catholic," someone who has grown up in the faith without making a mature personal commitment. The term enlivened her discussion of her religious beliefs. In sum, all essay writing must come alive to the reader.

II
Don't Forget the Verbs

Who likes to watch a fuzzy television screen? I don't. Neither do I enjoy reading essays that lack vividness, where the general, predictable, and vague statements blur into each other so much that my eyelids grow heavy and my grading pen weary.

Yes, the writer must make the words come alive to the reader through precise details. Beginning writers usually concentrate on nouns to achieve this; however, don't forget the verbs!

"Jump!"

The only part of speech that can exist by itself is the verb. It is the pulse of the sentence. So focus on verbs. Since they embody the heart of each clause, weak verbs guarantee weak sentences.

For instance, try to imagine the following: *he is, they will be, she was, I got, we had.*

Now imagine these: *he laughs, they dance, she dropped, I caught, we painted.*

What's the difference? The second group is so much easier to visualize.

Now reflect on the verbs in the following statements: He **did** the laundry. Too vague. He **washed** the laundry. Too common. He **folded** the laundry. Too predictable. How about, he **dropped** the laundry? A little better. He **stained** the laundry. Better. And finally, he **buried** the laundry? Hooked? The only difference in these statements rests on the verbs. Verbs can transform the sentence. They can transform your essay.

The most common weak verbs - to be, to do, to get, to have - will pop into your head constantly. Don't worry about them in your rough draft. They can be useful at times and impossible to avoid in certain cases. Just don't over use them. As you revise, systematically circle them. Note your dependence on them. Then, start over; remove as many as possible.

Sometimes, the verbs can be eliminated:

A. I *was* eight years old, when my family and I moved to Miami.

B. At eight years old, I relocated to Miami with my family.

Other times, they can be replaced with a stronger verb.

A. She *got* her suitcase ready for the trip.

B. She *stuffed* her suitcase for the trip.

From time to time, you will need to restructure entire sentences.

A. She *had* long brown hair. Her eyes *were* a striking green. She often *had* a strong effect on the people in her class.

B. With her long brown hair and striking green eyes, she often *attracted* the attention of her classmates.

Certain empty phrases often used in conversation contribute to weak verbs as well, so remove them as much as possible: it is important/necessary/essential that…, there is…, that is located…etc.

A. *There are* 25 students who are attending my yoga class *every day*.

B. Twenty five students regularly *attend* my yoga class.

The point: avoid using weak verbs as much as possible. Aim for verbs that show specific actions. Your essay will improve instantly.

III

Use Your Imagination

Born in Havana, Cuba, I was raised in the U.S.A. I now embrace my hybrid cultural background; however, throughout my twenties, being a cultural mutt became a source of doubt and confusion about my identity. In an essay in *The Miami Herald*, I published, "Culture can ground you, but it can also drown you." These two verbs, ground and drown, not only offer strong imagery, but also reveal to the reader, in a succinct way, the struggle between accepting and rejecting one's culture.

If the goal is to create vivid sharp images, details and strong action verbs (such as ground and drown) help you achieve this end, but so does the imagination. Culture does not literally ground you, like roots, or drown you, like a rip tide, but it can feel like it's doing both. This is called figurative language. Powerful comparisons like these add imagery and depth. A clever simile, an insightful analogy, or a witty pun, can enhance your descriptions, while contributing to the overall tone of your essay. One student in describing his compulsive eating as a lonely child wrote: "All the companions I needed were Oreos and Chips Ahoy." Another discussing bullying stated: "The girls treated me like a discarded bone."

Verbs can help here as well. Take the following sentence by one of my students: "We are catapulted through puberty, yet cling to the safety of our old familiar selves." The verbs "catapulted" and "cling" work figuratively by creating images that help us visualize the feelings a teenager experiences when thrust into young adulthood. Repeating the initial consonant sound, alliteration, also attracts attention to the verbs.

Comparisons are particularly useful when you are depicting something that is unfamiliar, complex, ambiguous, or abstract, like culture. By comparing your original object with something familiar, simpler or concrete, you can illuminate your points.

You have probably used metaphors, similes, and analogies in your high school creative writing classes, but they also play a role in composition classes. Strong essays scatter comparisons all throughout the text. In addition to enlivening individual images, they act as thread, connecting ideas. For example, in writing about a retiring colleague, I chose verbs associated with quilting. I wanted to create the sensation that he was sewing a life out of the pieces of his daily activities and friendships, without ever including the actual verb, to quilt. At one point, I stated, "I did not foresee how in time, we would bind to keep the edges of both our lives from fraying. With five minute scraps, we stitched our friendship."

Figurative language demands much from your imagination. It comes easier to some writers than others, but it's definitely worth the effort. Play around with similes, metaphors, analogies, personifications, but only keep the best: the ones that are fresh and insightful and that contribute to your essay's overall tone.

Don't use too many comparisons. That defeats the purpose. A few original ones work better than a bunch of clichés. If the comparison is overused, it loses its impact. Please, avoid common expressions such as "green with envy," "red as a tomato," and "home is where the heart is." The reader will be grateful.

If figurative language is not your strength, work on recalling relevant conversations or interesting statements, and sprinkle them throughout your essay. Did your grandmother have a favorite daily adage? Can you remember what your brother yelled before you punched him? Or recall a funny exchange between you and your teacher? Again, the purpose of including quotes or dialogue is to give life to your writing by stimulating the senses. Use them judiciously.

Of course, you can use pertinent and gripping quotes by famous individuals, especially in the introduction and the conclusion; however, make sure these flow easily in and out of your ideas. Avoid pasting on just any old quote you run across in the internet. It will feel contrived and inauthentic.

The objective of all these techniques - concrete details, strong action verbs, imaginative comparisons, relevant quotes – is to draw in your readers and keep them hooked to your essay until the end. You want to create an illusion so real that the reader forgets it's an essay.

Become a Team Player: Unity
Getting Your Game on for the Good of All

In a team sport, the team members must unite under a common goal. No one player should become a star at the expense of the others. The "star" might score a lot of points one game, but if the pattern continues, the rest of the players check out. In the end, the entire team loses out.

The same occurs in writing. Think of your thesis statement as your common goal for the entire essay. The rest of the paragraphs must support and relate back to that focus. In each body paragraph, the topic sentence provides the objective for that particular paragraph. All the details, examples, ideas, comparisons should flesh out the topic statement, which in turn connects back to the thesis in the introduction.

A simple example: let's say you're writing about suitable pets for condominium living. Your thesis may state: *As condominium living becomes more prevalent in major urban areas, certain types of pets make better choices.* Each subsequent paragraph would need to address this focus. Even though they make excellent pets on farms, you would not want to discuss larger breeds of dogs or ponies, unless briefly as negative examples. Instead, your main concentration should be on appropriate examples such as cats, small dogs, fish etc.

If the essay lacks unity, jumping around from one unrelated topic to another, the reader becomes confused. That's why it helps to regard the different parts of your essay as members of a team working together.

If you're told your essay lacks unity, then evaluate your thesis. Ask yourself, is the thesis too broad or too vague? If so, it will allow you to wander in too many directions throughout the body. Rein in your ideas. For that, you'll need to decide your specific destination.

On the other hand, perhaps your thesis statement is narrowing the focus too much. Recently, one student wanted to write a four page essay on one particular scene in a novel. Even though an important passage, it did not provide enough substance for her to sustain her focus effectively. I suggested she connect that scene to a later passage in the book that re-examined a related theme. Widening the focus allowed her to include additional elements and points of discussion without losing control over the unity. This occurs even more frequently in the body paragraphs.

Let's say one of your paragraphs on condominium pets deals with birds. If you run out of things to say about winged creatures and begin to discuss hamsters abruptly in the middle of the paragraph, you will confuse your reader. One option, besides eliminating all comments on hamsters, is to open up the topic sentence of that paragraph to include both birds and hamsters, perhaps by finding a commonality, such as "caged pets."

The bottom line: everything must belong and work together towards a clear and common goal. When you feel confident that the main idea of your essay works effectively and is clearly expressed at the end of the introduction, then move to your body paragraphs. Make sure each one maintains unity as it takes you one step closer to your destination. If you've made a wrong turn along the way, retrace your steps and continue. In other words, remove what doesn't belong and stay on target!

If every part of your essay follows the directions set out by the thesis and then the topic sentences, if every part of your essay works like a unified team, then you will achieve successful unity which translates into clarity for the reader.

Avoid Choppy Seas
Flow Smoothly through Your Ideas

Choppy seas do not make for a pleasant boat ride; choppy essays do not make for a pleasant read. You may have achieved unity in your ideas, but if you do not arrange these effectively, you will have created for your reader a rough ride. To avoid, make effective coherence a primary goal: a smooth flow from one point to another.

Start by reviewing your **organization**. Memories, ideas, examples, facts do not come to mind in a logical fashion. After brainstorming or free writing, step back and think about your points. Find the most reasonable way to present them to your reader.

If referring to time, arrange your points in chronological order: from morning, to afternoon, to evening; from birth, to adolescence, to adulthood; from the 14th, to the 17th, to the 20th century. What if you want to include a flashback? That's fine, as long as you control the shift and it's clear that you have altered the order for a reason. Randomly combining details is never a good strategy.

If you're describing something spatially, find a logical way to move around the object. From outside in, from downstairs up, from right to left. For instance, if you are recreating a car accident, start by describing the intersection and the cars involved, before you mention the blood in the back seat, even though that may be what you remember most. Figure out what's most logical for your reader; don't just throw in all the objects and hope they land in the right place. Become the master of your essay.

The same applies to ideas. Organize them from general to specific or vice versa; from most important to least important or the reverse. Create tension with your ideas. It will sustain the reader more effectively.

Beware, you can logically organize your ideas, and still have poor coherence. If that's the case, then you probably lack effective **transitions**. A student once said that transitions separate ideas. He probably made that assumption since transitions work well at the beginning or the end of a paragraph. It must have appeared to him as if the transitions were separating the paragraphs. In fact, transitions do the opposite. They **link** them.

Writing is about making connections. Through transitions, the writer reveals the associations between major points. Transitions at the end of a paragraph anticipate what's coming. The statement, "Cats are not the only good choices for condominium living," lets the reader expect a shift to a different pet. On the other hand, transitions can drag down the topic from the previous paragraph, linking it to the new topic. For instance, beginning with the topic sentence, "In addition to cats, small dogs can also make first-rate companions in small quarters," lets the reader easily make a new connection.

In the same way, revealing the relationships between individual sentences within the paragraphs is indispensable. Use sentence connectors to disclose the associations between specific ideas, examples, or facts. You can achieve this through coordination (joining independent clauses to make a compound sentence) and subordination (joining two clauses, one subordinated, to make a complex sentence). In other words, continue to show the reader the links. Don't leave it up to the reader to figure out why you are providing certain information. Expose the connections.

To achieve this, find your short choppy simple sentences and identify the relationships between them. Is one sentence contradicting the previous one or adding more information? Is it providing an example of what you stated earlier? Or is it showing the result of what was just explained? Figure it out; then combine the sentences with a coordinating (for, and, nor, but, or, yet, so) or subordinating conjunction (after, although, because, before, even though, if, since, until) or adverb. Keep a list of the most common conjunctive adverbs handy any time you sit down to write, as a reminder: accordingly, also, anyway, besides, certainly, furthermore, however, indeed, likewise, meanwhile, still, moreover, nevertheless, similarly, therefore. With practice, linking ideas will become natural to you.

Warning: beginning writers connect most sentences with a simple "and," which is easy, but not good enough. "And" does not clarify the specific relationship between the ideas; consequently, it does not help the reader to predict what is coming, like a "however" or a "similarly."

Knowing what to expect, helps the reader to navigate more smoothly from X to Y. For example, when you write "X; consequently, Y," the reader can anticipate that Y is a result of X, as opposed to "X; moreover, Y," which indicates additional information will be provided. In sum, do the hard work of choosing the appropriate conjunctions to disclose the associations between the sentences.

In addition to effective organization and transitions, the repetition of **key terms** throughout the text, as well as **parallelism**, will help improve the flow. Parallelism, sustaining a pattern in the sentence structures, is particularly effective. It allows the reader to anticipate the future, thus increasing coherence and adding emphasis. (See page 61.)

All of these techniques are essential to effective smooth communication, so use them to avoid choppy seas!

The Secret to a Happy Essay is Consistency
Choose Well and Commit

Do you have friends who love your jokes one day, yet are offended by them the next day? How do they make you feel? Confused, insecure, aggravated? The same occurs with writing.

Most of us like people and things we can count on. They let us know what to expect and help us feel satisfied when that expectation is fulfilled. That's why we are attracted to consistent patterns.

Inconsistencies in the writing make the reader feel bewildered and frustrated. For the reader to trust you, you must be reliable. Part of that comes from constancy in every aspect of the essay, from overall tone to specific verb tenses.

Choose a tone - thoughtful and academic, satirical and tongue-in-cheek, or challenging and argumentative – it's up to you. Once you begin to write in that tone, however, stick to it.

The same applies to the diction. Do you want to use a formal, semi-formal, or casual conversational language? If you are not sure, discuss it with your instructor. Most academic essays work best with a semi-formal style which uses direct unadorned language and avoids contractions and clichés. In addition, unless you have a good reason for using it, such as within a direct quote, stay away from slang or jargon, which may be offensive and/or unfamiliar to your readers, including your instructor. Like with tone, be consistent in your diction throughout the essay.

After tone and diction, review your content - your ideas, examples, arguments, analogies - to make sure you are not contradicting yourself in any way. Make sure you haven't lost your way in the process of developing your thoughts.

Once you have revised these major elements for consistency, zero in on more specific items, such as verb tenses, person and number.

Verb tenses: check that you are not switching randomly between tenses. It's one thing to begin in the present and turn to the past when you shift into a memory or flashback. It's another to slip into a different tense without even realizing it, such as in:

My father turns to me and whispered.

This happens most commonly to beginning writers when they recount a memory in the present tense. It can be done and certainly adds immediacy to the text; however, it is a dangerous strategy since writers will often slip between tenses without noticing. This confuses the readers and should be avoided.

Parts of Speech: review each sentence to verify that the nouns, verbs and pronouns all agree in number (singular or plural) and person (first/I, second/you, third/he, she).

For example, a student essay stated:

Hemingway always portrays a tough guy in his books as they are struggling adversity.

Instead he should have said:

*Hemingway always portrays tough **guys**.*

In another instance, the student wrote:

His classmates often forget to bring their book to class.

He should have said:

*His classmates often forget to bring their **books** to class.*

From these minor grammar issues to the broader elements, make sure to revise everything, yes everything, in your essay for consistency. Sustaining patterns will definitely enhance your writing by adding clarity and ease.

Climbing Your Personal Mt. Everest

There's No Turning Back

Few of us will attempt to climb Mt. Everest in our lifetimes. Nevertheless, we will pursue similarly difficult goals that will require the best of us: discipline, perseverance, wisdom, and commitment. For many of us, our relationships are our personal Mt. Everest.

A good relationship demands constancy, and much more. Couples stay together, in spite of unexpected imperfections, economic problems, illnesses, annoying in-laws, new baby sleepless nights. Why? Is it because they love each other? Sure, but frankly it takes more than "being in love" to sustain two individuals through one adversity after another. It takes commitment.

People in long term relationships understand that life's journey together will challenge their resolve, but they make a commitment to work hard. To them it's worth the effort to hold on to a companion they can trust and value.

View your essay as a companion. Once you've started the process, give it a chance and keep working with it.

Every essay has a turning point when the writing rebels. Sometimes it's due to a lack of motivation because you were assigned the subject matter, but, even if you have chosen the topic yourself, it can still suddenly become difficult to continue. Maybe you've run out of details or ideas. Maybe you're just too tired or too exasperated to keep going. Everything you have written begins to sound incoherent or insignificant. That's exactly the point when the temptation to switch topics will strike.

Like in a struggling relationship, a new subject can hold much promise. If I can just start over, you'll think, this new essay will be easier. Guess what? It's never easy. Each essay, like each relationship, poses unique challenges. The task of turning an early quick draft into a brilliantly effective final essay is always demanding and draining, regardless of the topic. So give in to it.

In nine out of ten cases, you will reach that spot again when you will feel like the mountain is too steep to climb; again, you'll second guess yourself and look for a way around it. This can continue forever. Some of my students switch subjects two or three times without making progress. At some point, you must accept and pursue the tasks that all writing requires, or give it up. The latter means no essay, so you might as well make up your mind sooner than later. Commit and stick to it! The rewards at the end are always worth it.

Someone once said, "If you want an interesting relationship, stay married." The same applies to writing. "If you want an interesting essay, stay with it."

Polish it until it glows.

OMG! TMI!

Tighten *Your Sentences*

In writing, less means more. Beginning writers often use too many words to explain what could be stated in fewer. Instead of saying *the hospital employee,* they write *the person who works at the hospital.*

So?

Unnecessary words impact writing **negatively**. They dilute the power of the images and ideas, just like excess water dilutes the taste of juice. In other words, they make the writing tasteless and FLAT! What a shame to come up with vivid details and stimulating perspectives, only to put your reader to sleep with excessive wordiness.

If your writing suffers from wordiness, overcoming this problem will dramatically improve your writing.

For example, a student recently wrote: "My teenage years were becoming full of someone who chose not to express emotions, to sympathize, to pity, and to let anyone in." I reread her sentence several times before I could decipher its meaning. Her wordiness hindered the clarity and power of her ideas. Instead, she could have said: "I became a closed off teenager unable or unwilling to express emotions such as sympathy or pity."

Wordiness can result from laziness. Instead of looking up the precise word to make your point, you use more common vague language because it occurs to you quickly.

For example, students often say "he *went through a lot of* challenges," instead of "he *experienced numerous* challenges;" or "I *thought I was going* to find him in the kitchen," instead of "I *expected* to find him in the kitchen."

Lack of revision also leads to wordiness:

"My boyfriend and I met because of our little sisters; they were best friends in middle school," a student wrote. (Tip: notice the weak verbs; they can serve as a warning system.)

The student could have combined ideas more effectively by tightening the sentence and simultaneously removing the weak verb "were" in the second clause: "My boyfriend and I met through our little sisters, best friends in middle school."

In fact, wordiness can lead to confusing constructions:

One student wrote: "I never gave much thought as to how much destruction a small note could create;" instead of "I never considered the potential damage caused by a small note."

Long awkward wordy sentences should be broken down, simplified, and then reconnected more effectively.

Sometimes, tightening a sentence can be achieved easily, by removing a word(s); other times, however, you might need to restructure an entire sentence or even two. You need to play around with the language and the sentence, until you succeed.

A quick list of concrete suggestions to help you avoid wordiness:

1) Avoid weak verbs when possible, especially:
to be, to have, to do, and to get (in all their forms)

For example, instead of "I made a decision *to go into* the Coast Guard," write: "I made a decision *to join* the Coast Guard."

Unbelievably, some students can tell an entire story with only one verb such as in:

"I *got* my clothes on, *got* into my car, and *got* my friend. When we *got* to the party, we *got* to see old friends from high school. Unfortunately, we *got* drunk. That night, I *got* so happy when I *got* home at last."

Instead he could have stated:

"After *dressing*, I *picked up* my friend and we *drove* to the party where we *reconnected* with high school friends. Unfortunately, we *consumed* too much alcohol. Afterwards, I *felt* relieved to finally arrive at home."

2) Avoid wordy expressions such as:

There are...there is...

It is important that...it is essential that...it is necessary that...which is located...that is above...which is utilized...

They are unnecessary and usually used as fillers in verbal communication to give the speaker more time to think. In writing, they should be removed when possible.

3) Avoid familiar, yet vague, words such as:

really, very, quite, special, totally, fairly, actually, nice, *even* beautiful.

Instead, use a specific detail or a metaphor. For instance, instead of *very tall*, say *he's 6ft11* or *as tall as a giraffe*. Both of these options offer more specificity and thus create more interest for the reader.

4) Beware of adverbs and adjectives. Find the precise verb or noun to depict what you want to say.

Instead of *he spoke softly*, write *he whispered.*
Instead of *he ran quickly*, say he *dashed.*
Instead of the *small child*, use the *toddler.*

5) Avoid redundancies such as the *round* ball, the *free* gift, the *dead* corpse, the *month* of July, the *color* green, the thought *in his mind*, the feeling *in his heart*, or the employee *who works here*. They are not needed and further dilute your words.

6) When you have a choice, use the shortest, most direct version of phrases such as: now (for "at the present time"), since (for "due to the fact that"), to (for "in order to") etc.

The longer expressions don't make you sound more sophisticated. They make you sound like you are trying to sound more sophisticated and in the process detract from the power of your writing.

Beware of using "fancy" words or phrases from a thesaurus. They may lengthen your sentences unnecessarily, or worse, confuse the reader because of inappropriate usage. Using a thesaurus to jolt your memory toward a familiar word in order to add variety is fine. Too many students, however, use badly chosen expressions just to sound "like a writer."

7) Combine ideas/sentences to avoid needlessly repeating yourself.

Instead of "My mother is turning 57. She was born in the month of October of 1954," write "My mother, born in 1954, turns 57 this October."
Instead of "The narrator felt he had to return home. He decided to return home because he wanted to be part of the reconstruction process," write "The narrator felt the need to return home to participate in the reconstruction process."

8) Avoid the passive voice because it usually lengthens your sentences unnecessarily.

Sometimes, we use the passive construction on purpose, for example when we say: "My car was stolen" (since we don't know the thief's identity) or "The stereo broke" (because we don't know who or what caused it).
On the other hand, when there is a clear subject, the passive construction will add wordiness and make your sentences drag (like in many textbooks). Instead of writing "The teacher's request for silence was ignored by the unruly students," say "The unruly students ignored the teacher's request for silence." In addition to shortening the sentence, the latter version adds clarity.

In conclusion, tightening your sentences will energize your writing. Don't be afraid to trim the fat. Less is more, so be ruthless.

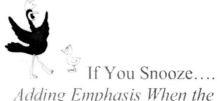

If You Snooze....
Adding Emphasis When the Going Gets Boring

As you tighten your sentences, consider which ideas, facts, or details you want to emphasize. Make those stand out.

In talking, we achieve this by slowing down or raising our voices. The contrast in speed, rhythm, volume, or intonation can draw in the listener's attention. There's nothing more boring than a monotone teacher. I'm sure you've had a few. The instructor can be a genius, but if he or she talks endlessly, at the same speed, tone or volume, we can't help but lose interest and tune out. The same will happen to your reader if you do not add emphasis and variety. They work together to keep your reader alert.

Ask yourself, what is important in each sentence that deserves the most attention?

Evaluate every single sentence? YES!

Consider each sentence like a section in a large watercolor. Can the artist carefully paint two thirds of the canvas, then sloppily brush the remaining blank space because he or she is tired or rushed? Absolutely not. The painter must respect every fragment of the canvas.

Likewise, the author must review every sentence in the manuscript. Rewriting takes time. That's why you should save 40% of your time for revision. But not just for checking grammar, spelling and punctuation. Consider those last. Before then, much work still needs to be done.

Assuming you have already tightened your sentences, additional techniques can further invigorate them:

1) **Locate your most important points at the end of the sentence**. Every sentence is a tiny story. Build tension toward the end. The end of the sentence attracts the most attention. Don't waste it. The second best location is the start of your sentence. Never hide important details in the middle!

For example, instead of "I bought a pair of leather pants for my 80 year old grandmother's birthday," try, "For her 80th birthday, I bought my grandmother a pair of leather pants."

What a difference the order makes! The most interesting aspect of this sentence is the fact that an 80 year old grandmother would wear leather pants. That's why these 2 details work more effectively when placed at the end and the beginning of the sentence.

2) **Use parallelism**; it not only enhances coherence, but adds emphasis. Repeat a similar structure two or three times; more defeats the purpose by becoming stale. Parallelism adds weight to your points. Because of the parallel structures, the readers will anticipate what's coming while expecting each new statement to increase in importance. This will keep them attentive. For example:

"What is it about adolescence that makes us hyper sensitive about our looks? What is it about adolescence that makes the simplest decision feel monumental? What is it about adolescence that makes us question the very essence of ourselves?"

3) **Use active voice** more than passive voice. (See page 59.)

4) **Include variety in sentence structure**. If you are not purposely creating parallel structures, then you should not overuse any one type of construction. One of my students was addicted to a similar structure. "As I felt I didn't belong, I closed myself off from friends." "As I started to gain weight, my self-esteem plummeted." "As I lost confidence, I made alcohol my new companion." Alone, each of these sentences works, but too many sentences with the same structure become monotonous and a nuisance for the reader. Try to identify your "writing preferences" and avoid overusing them.

5) Even **in sentence length, add variety**. All types of sentences exist: simple or complex ones; short or long ones.

In academic writing, aim for complex longer sentences, but sprinkle a few shorter, simpler, ones here and there; otherwise, you'll sound like a textbook. Too many short sentences, on the other hand, will make you sound choppy and infantile. Find the balance. Remember, that the emphasis comes from the contrast. After a few longer sentences, the short direct one will attract attention. That's the one to choose for your significant points. One of my students effectively used variety in sentence length in the following:

"It has been two months since I've seen my car, my shiny black dodge, tainted by my own immaturity. One night on vacation in Orlando, I wanted to buy food after a long night of drinking without considering what could happen to me. I felt invincible."

6) **Be creative**. Don't be afraid to use a question as a transition, a dash as punctuation, or figurative language as an attention device. Take risks. Have some fun.

The same student cleverly added later on: "My ego was totaled along with my car. They both needed some serious repairs."

In sum, be prepared to play around with your words and your sentences. Without emphasis and variety, your writing will feel stale and boring.

Detangle Your Sentences
Cleaning up messes

At times, you collect so many brilliant ideas and examples that you fear they'll spill over. So you quickly gather them in one long tangled mess of a sentence. Or at least that's what it feels like. Tangled sentences lack clarity. They can result from different reasons; however, the effect is the same: confusion.

It took me a few minutes to decipher what Jerome meant in the following sentence:

"When I was learning about his childhood, it was the starting point of me developing a knowledge of empathy and gratitude." This convoluted sentence needed tightening, but also untangling.

In fact, the student meant to state: "Learning about his childhood helped me to develop empathy and gratitude."

To avoid tangled sentences such as this one, you first need to recognize them. To help you, read your essay a loud to yourself or to another person. Listen for twisted phrases and drawn out ideas. If you are lucky, you can solve the problem by removing wordiness or adding punctuation, such as a period or a semi-colon to two independent ideas crashing into each other.

More often, tangled sentences are the result of over-stuffed sentences. Too many ideas or examples jumbled together. If that's the case, break apart your sentence. Write two or three clearer shorter sentences to replace the one drawn out tortuous one.

One student recently wrote:

"This led me to seek out for a role model and indeed I soaked up the words and actions of icons such as Muhammad Ali, Richard Branson, and Mahatma Gandhi and any person one can say had a profound influence on this planet so they shaped the overall blueprint of the person I hoped to become." Wow! That's a mouthful.

I suggested the student remove wordiness and break apart the sentence:

"This led me to seek a role model, so I soaked up the influence of icons such as Muhammad Ali, Richard Branson, and Mahatma Gandhi. They shaped the blueprint of the person I hoped to become."

Other times, tangled sentences are the result of mixed constructions; you begin with a structure that doesn't match the rest, so it doesn't make sense. For example:

"By looking at the relationship between Abigail Adams and John Adams, it can show that their partnership represented a central aspect of his political life." What?!

Try instead: "The relationship between Abigail Adams and John Adams shows how their partnership was essential to his political life."

If necessary, pull apart longer sentences. Make sure each shorter sentence has clarity; then reconnect them. In short, make sure each sentence, whether short or long, simple or complex, has clarity!

Punctuation Sweat
The Pause that Refreshes

When I review rules of punctuations on the board, students look at me as if I were explaining tools of torture. In fact, I dislike teaching these rules as much as they hate following them. It's so much easier to intuitively decide what works best; however, if students are not avid readers, which creates intuitive writers, they must apply punctuation rules methodically.

Humans first started communicating orally. They say it wasn't until the 4th millennium BC that written communication emerged. By then, human culture had become too complex for transmitting information exclusively through memory.

Written communication at first consisted of symbols that represented objects and eventually sounds. As Aristotle declared, "Speech is the representation of the experiences of the mind and writing is the representation of speech" (*On Interpretation*). In speaking, as in music, pauses (silences) are an integral part of the communication. The symbols for these pauses are what we commonly call punctuation. Punctuation evolved with time. It contributes to the rhythm and intonation of the language, but it is particularly helpful to clarify meaning.

For this reason, it helps to understand the different functions of punctuation marks. Depending on the length and complexity of a sentence, punctuations will vary to designate different lengths in pauses.

Generally the comma denotes the shortest pause, the semicolon next, then the colon, and finally the period. Think of them like the traffic lights of your sentences. They were not designed to torment you, but to assist the reader.

Some fun classic examples illustrate the necessary role punctuation plays in providing clarity:

"Woman, without her man, is nothing."

"Woman, without her, man is nothing."

One simple comma placement completely alters the meaning.

Or take the old joke: A panda walks into a café. He orders a sandwich, eats it, then draws a gun and proceeds to fire it at the other patrons. "Why?" asks the confused, surviving waiter amidst the carnage, as the panda makes towards the exit. The panda produces a badly punctuated wildlife manual and tosses it over his shoulder. "Well, I'm a panda," he says, at the door. "Look it up." The waiter turns to the relevant entry in the manual and, sure enough, finds an explanation. "Panda: Large black-and-white bear-like mammal, native to China. Eats, shoots and leaves." (*Eats, Shoots and Leaves* is also the title of a best seller by Lynne Truss which reviews the rules of punctuation in a humorous way.)

The truth is the rules of English change because language changes. Rules slow down the changes, but eventually widespread usage forces the alteration. Until a rule does change, though, students need to be familiar with it. Teachers point out the punctuation mistakes because in current "Standard English," that is, the English accepted among professionals, these errors interfere with effective communication to convey one's meaning. And effective communication is the goal.

If you feel insecure about your mastery of punctuation, you can turn to many handbooks, grammar books, or on-line sources for specific rules, but here are a few general comments that will help you with punctuation.

The punctuation mark most misused by beginning writers is **the comma**. They use the comma where it doesn't belong, yet don't use the comma where it is really needed.

Commas help to group ideas together or separate them within a sentence.

They cannot be used, however, to combine two independent clauses. They do not call for a long enough pause for the reader to absorb the first idea before moving to the next. If you use the comma alone between independent ideas, you are creating a common sentence error: *a comma-splice.*

On the other hand, beginning writers don't use commas enough in numerous necessary situations. Among these, the most useful would include:

1) To separate an introductory phrase or clause from the main subject and verb of the sentence. "As an introverted teenager, I detested school."

2) To separate items in a series. "Honesty, determination, and perseverance bolstered Adam's strongest asset, his inquiring mind." Use it even if it's a series of clauses. "By the end of the semester, John improved the most, Mercedes became the most extroverted, and Simon showed the most ambition."

3) To separate two groups of words joined by conjunctions such as: and, but, yet, or, so. Place the comma before the coordinating conjunction. "Write your essay quickly, but revise it slowly."

4) To separate nonrestrictive, nonessential, items from the main sentence. In other words, items not necessary to understand the main sentence. "Her grandmother, who flew in from Cuba, will be staying the month."

5) To set off interjections or quotation marks. Carlos said, "I refuse to follow."

Unlike the comma, the **semicolon** demands a longer pause, so it can be used to link independent clauses related to each other.

You can use it by itself: "It looks stormy over the coastline; I'm definitely not going to the beach today;" or with conjunctive adverbs, "It looks stormy over the coastline; nevertheless, I'm still going to the beach." It depends if you want to speed up or slow down the sentence.

In a series, where the items include a comma, you should use the semi-colon as a way to separate each item. "He finally agreed to pay for the prop, made especially for the event; the costume, altered to fit him; and the caterer."

An underused handy punctuation mark is the **colon**. Most beginning writers use it to introduce a series of items; however, it can also be useful to introduce a second clause which provides clarification or further development of the first. "The young man felt betrayed by his sister: she ran away from home without even saying goodbye."

In addition to periods, commas, semi-colon and colons, you should be familiar with the proper usage of apostrophes, quotation marks, parenthesis, and dashes. If you are not, review them in your grammar sources. Look at them as collaborators (not enemies) to assist you in adding clarity and emphasis to your projects.

Dress for Success
Appropriate Diction/Word Choices

"Clothes make the man. Naked people have little or no influence in society," said Mark Twain.

Luckily I don't bump into naked students as I walk my college hallways. From time to time, I do encounter students wearing shorts or tops exposing more than I care to see, or sporting inappropriate undershirts, hoods, crack revealing low riders, or pajama-like bottoms. What are they thinking? I ask myself.

If you attend college, you're headed for professional success. No? That entails thinking of clothes in a new way. Part of maturing professionally involves determining the suitable attire for any given situation: a classroom, an office, a restaurant, a courtroom.

Are you considering the legal, corporate, or academic fields? Start getting used to jackets. Maybe you prefer a medical field: physical therapy, physician assistant, nurse, doctor? Scrubs will become a familiar word. Are you considering teaching or dentistry? Think about comfortable shoes! Every occupation demands proper attire.

In truth, before you can even launch your career, you'll need to survive the interview process. That's when you'll really begin to dress for success. Jeans, wrinkled shirts, sneakers or flip flop sandals will not make a good impression. Choosing the right clothing for an interview demonstrates good judgment, a positive personality trait your future employer will appreciate.

Likewise, writing demands good judgment in selecting the appropriate word choices. It's important to appeal to your readers, not offend or alienate them. Start by thinking about your audience. Who will be reading your essay? Your instructor? Your classmates? What are their ages? Their gender? Their level of education? Take into account all these factors in determining your diction.

As discussed earlier, most beginning writers depend too much on oral communication which relies heavily on regionalisms, dialects, colloquialisms, even slang - all variations on the communication by a narrow group in their particular region, state, city, ethnicity, age, or even neighborhood. These expressions tend to be spirited and colorful which are positive qualities. It's fun to say, "He refused to disappear, like a floating turd;" or "He stunk like a skunk;" or "La Vaquita" (the closest Farm Stores to a Cuban American household). The problem is that readers might become offended or confused.

For example, in Miami, where a large number of residents speak Spanish, or are at least familiar with it, the writer might get away with using the term a "midnight" sandwich, a literal translation of the popular and delicious ham, pork and cheese "medianoche" sandwich; even so, the writer runs a risk of being misunderstood.

To avoid mix-ups, it's a good idea to keep the wording semi-formal, without slang or colloquial diction, but avoid the other extreme of using pretentious language. Some of my honors students suffer from this ailment. They have acquired the habit of impressing the reader (most likely their teacher) with words that sounds flamboyant and complex, which are in fact unnatural and convoluted, such as "due to the fact that" or "I hydrated myself extensively before proceeding toward the beach." Moreover, this kind of long-winded terminology can lead to mixed constructions or a pompous tone.

Something else to consider is how you refer to a person's ethnicity. Because so much of the United States is populated by individuals from different backgrounds, be careful to use the standard accepted by educated speakers and writers of English. This may change of course, but all you can do is make an effort to be respectful, accurate, and relevant. The bottom line is to consider how a member of a particular group would perceive the way you are referring to him or her.

Gender is a sensitive issue as well. In the past, male terms were accepted to refer to the general group; this is no longer the case, so you should avoid it. Instead, consider using terms such as: human being or humanity for man or mankind, ancestor for forefather, police officer for policeman, mail carrier for mailman, work force for man power, chair or head for chairman.

One of the trickier problems is avoiding the generic "he" pronoun without having to constantly refer to *him or her, his or her*, which quickly gets annoying. The easiest solution is to use the plural.

Instead of saying: "*Each student* should always bring *his or her* textbook to class," write "*Students* should always bring *their* textbooks to class."

You could also eliminate the pronoun altogether when possible. As in, "Students should always bring *the* textbook to class."

A few other terms to avoid include jargons and euphemisms. Jargons are specialized words from a specific field, such as legal, medical, financial, or scientific, that may be unfamiliar to the target reader. Euphemisms, on the other hand, use alternate language to avoid describing something directly. They often sound contrived, but more importantly, they can be used to circumvent the true meaning, even in cases to mislead.

Examples of euphemisms include: passing, instead of dying; downsizing, instead of firing; collateral damage, instead of casualties; or ethnic cleansing, instead of genocide.

Finally, remember to stay away from those tempting clichés that offer familiarity. My students love to write: "a diamond in the rough," "lasted an eternity," "eats like a pig" or "stuck between a rock and a hard plate." Overused expressions like these have lost much of their initial impact, so use them sparingly

In the end, the goal is to provide interesting language, that is clear and appropriate for the situation. To that end, choose words that are precise and direct, unadorned or faddish. Like in selecting your professional wardrobe, make sure you include language that appeals to your target audience and will not make you look or sound out of place!

Know Your Subjects
The King and Queen of English Rules

Sentences make up essays, so understanding how they work improves your writing. This is particularly true for English which possesses less syntactical flexibility than let's say Spanish. For instance, in Spanish, the subject of a sentence can easily be omitted, while in English, the subject can never be left out.

In fact, the sentence is the basic unit of all writing. It requires two main elements: the verb and its subject. Think of them as the king and queen of each sentence.

The heart of a sentence is the verb which conveys an action (*to laugh, to spit, to dance*) or a state of being (*to be, to seem*). It's the only part of speech that can stand alone. A simple command, such as *Speak!* can function as a complete sentence; however, unless the verb is a command (where the subject is understood to be *you*), an English sentence *always* requires a subject.

The subject is the person, place, thing, or idea that is *doing* or *being* something to which the verb refers. The subject is usually the doer of the action: ***Marcos*** *ate the leftover pizza*. In some cases, however, where passive voice is used instead of active, the subject can be the recipient of the action: *The leftover **pizza** was eaten by Marcos*. In either case, a subject is necessary. Sometimes, pronouns will stand for the nouns (it, he, she, they, we...) as the subject. *He ate the pizza*. You cannot say "Ate a lot," as you would in Spanish, "Comio mucho."

Words that describe nouns are called adjectives (clumsy, tall, handsome, gray). Those that describe verbs, as well as other adverbs, adjectives, and phrases, are called adverbs. They usually describe how, where, when or why something happens (carefully, here, rarely, accidentally).

A simple sentence includes one verb and its subject, regardless of how many adjectives or adverbs: The new *student arrived* late to class. Simple sentences offer much clarity.

Nevertheless, a sentence can also contain more than one verb and its accompanying subject. Each combination of subject and verb is considered a clause.

Clauses can be independent, meaning that they can stand alone and be understood, or dependent. Dependent clauses rely on the primary clause for meaning, so they cannot stand alone, as in: *although they lost their house*. In combination, multiple clauses can make up one sentence.

If both clauses are independent, joined by a conjunction (*and, but, yet, nor, etc.*) the sentence is considered a compound sentence; however, if an independent clause is combined with a dependent one, then the sentence is considered complex.

1) Compound sentences emphasize the ideas in both clauses **equally**.

The student parked in the garage, and he rushed to his first class.

2) Complex sentences allow you to play with the dynamics of your writing, like in a musical composition. They allow you to emphasize some points at the expense of others. A dependent clause can be connected to a main independent clause by a subordinating conjunction (*although, because, which, as if, even though, etc.*) to form the complex sentence:

Since the student was late for class again, he parked illegally. In this case, the independent clause (*he parked illegally*) attracts more attention.

You need to decide what type of sentence best serves your purpose, but your essay should include a combination of all these types of sentences in a variety of lengths. Appreciating how the elements of a sentence work helps you to manipulate them more effectively as you revise for clarity and emphasis.

Other rules about capitalization, possession, abbreviations, and spelling are also important, but much simpler to grasp and easily accessible. If your instructor has marked your essays for those types of problems, then find a pattern. Make note of your weaknesses and take advantage of a wealth of on-line information to check your errors. Don't ignore them or hope they'll disappear by themselves. By now, your errors have probably become bad habits which you need to reprogram. In a few seconds you can clarify any grammar doubt. Just Google it!

Prove It!
Persuading Your Reader

Doctored magazine shots, misleading TV commercials, negative political ads, twitter lies. Technology has made us more easily susceptible to manipulation, but truthfully, since the time of Ancient Greece, learned individuals have studied the nature of language and culture in order to sway others to their point of view. This included identifying which words would entertain, impress, or persuade an audience.

This rhetorical knowledge combined with current data on brain function and psychology, plus the new technologies, have increased exponentially the power to influence and even manipulate an audience.

For a writer, eager to win over the reader, this knowledge is indispensable to grasp how human beings are persuaded through writing. In fact, whether you are writing about a controversial topic or not, all writing demands a certain level of persuasion.

To start, don't underestimate the role of tone in persuading your reader. Tone is the underlying attitude you hold toward your subject matter and readers, as revealed through the language. Because tone can motivate or discourage readers, it's important to find a balance in the writing that is objective, respectful, and professional. This does not mean dull and boring. On the contrary, it means open-minded and flexible, even lighthearted, if appropriate to the topic.

Think of relatives whose advice you'd never seek. Are they opinionated, overbearing, arrogant, or obstinate? We tend to avoid those types of individuals, so you certainly don't want to sound like them - condescending or self-righteous. It's best not to come on too strong nor mock those who would disagree with you. Instead of convincing your readers, you will only alienate them.

On the other hand, individuals who lack assertiveness, command of the subject matter, or decisiveness do not inspire confidence. We usually avoid their advice as well. For instance, repeating "in my personal opinion" too often, or using helping verbs such as would, could, or may, will weaken your tone by making you sound insecure. Even if you are not 100% sure of your assertions, you must sound like it.

Many of my two year college students have trouble convincing their parents why they should move away to finish their four year degree. In approaching mom and dad, I suggest, they sound mature, assertive, and knowledgeable. If they come on too aggressive or sound like a five year old whining about how "this is MY life," they will not inspire their parents' confidence. Likewise in writing, an appropriate tone helps to draw in the reader and establish credibility. Readers must believe you are unbiased, but also informed.

To establish your tone, it helps to understand your audience. To arouse confidence, it helps to know your topic well, from all sides; that way you can respectfully address other relevant points of views and establish common ground.

For instance, in convincing mom and dad of the merits of going away to college, I advise my students to consider their parents 'concerns. These may include: how to pay for room and board, in addition to tuition; how to be safe; how to remain focused on studies; how to manage at home without their child's support. These are legitimate points the students must anticipate.

If they have done the research and feel calm, the students can validate the parents' fears. Then, address each of them with the information acquired about financial aid, part-time jobs, cheap rents, buddy systems, cell phones; in addition, they can offer additional data to impress upon the parents why this experience will help the students academically, professionally and personally in the long run. Finally, I suggest reminding mom and dad that both parents and students share a common goal: to find the best path towards a successful future. In the same informed, confident, and understanding way you approach parents, you must approach your readers.

Tone will only take you so far; supporting your opinions with effective proof is the main way to pursuade parents or readers. You should use a combination of concrete details, examples, facts, statistics, experts' opinions, testimonies, values, beliefs, and analogies, depending on the topic. Coming up with these will demand that you generate numerous details and ideas, as well as sufficient research.

If you're writing about a personal event, trying to pursuade your reader of its impact on your life, you need to provide numerous precise sensory details – for vividness and authenticiy – as well as to analyze all the ramifications of the incident. A topic such as this relies primarily on concrete details, personal testimony and beliefs.

If then again, you're trying to pursuade your readers of the negative effects of processed foods, in an expository essay, you would use facts, statistics, expert opinions and examples. The thesis will dictate the necessary type of evidence. Familiarizing yourself with your readers (age, gender, ethnicity, economic and educational level) also helps you select facts, examples, and values most relevant to them.

Regardless of the topic, ample preparation will provide you with the objectivity, assurance, and compassion you need to inspire your readers' confidence in you. Then you can appeal to their logic with good research and emotions with compelling examples. That's how you pursuade!

Hear No Evil, See No Evil, Write No Evil
Thinking Logically

True or false? Something can be valid but not true. True. How?

Thinking logically doesn't always equate with finding the truth, but it's a start. Two methods of logic used to arrive at a conclusion based on information assumed to be true are inductive and deductive reasoning. Both are used in research. Both have limitations.

Inductive reasoning uses specific observations to make generalizations. When a toddler touches a glowing light bulb, he makes a mental note of the burning pain. After experiencing the same outcome a few times, he concludes that bright light bulbs cause pain and avoids touching them! The child is using his inductive reasoning. Inductive reasoning is the basis for most of our learning as we experience life. From specific instances, we formulate general conclusions which may be strong or weak, depending on the number of examples witnessed.

The problem with this kind of reasoning is that it cannot be used as evidence of fact, unless one has experienced 100% of the possible samples. In most cases, however, we make a leap to a conclusion after witnessing only some examples. If that's the case, the conclusion is not absolute. In fact, the wider the leap, the less probable the conclusion is correct.

Unfortunately, most stereotypes are based on inconclusive inductive reasoning. In Miami, you often hear people say, Cubans are so loud! Inductive reasoning has taken action. After noticing several loud Cubans, someone concludes: All Cubans are loud. Two problems: first, perhaps the quiet ones have gone unnoticed. Second, even if many are loud, it takes a huge leap to conclude all 11 million plus Cubans are loud. Ironically, the less we know about someone or something, the bigger the leaps we take. It's human nature to simplify. The danger rests in over-simplification which often results from inductive reasoning.

On the other hand, deductive reasoning uses a general premise to arrive at a specific conclusion. It can be helpful in moving us from broad observations to particular assumptions. Whether the conclusion is true, however, depends on the general premise. That is why deductive reasoning can be based on valid reasoning yet be untrue.

Take the case of the loud Cubans again. If one generalizes that all Cubans are loud based on limited observations and then meets one Cuban, Marisela, deductive reasoning will arrive at a valid, yet faulty, conclusion: If all Cubans are loud, and Marisela is Cuban, then deductive reasoning tells us that Marisela must be loud. In fact, Marisela is not loud, even though yes she's Cuban. The conclusion is valid based on the generalization provided, but because the major premise is not true, the specific conclusion is also not true.

Inductive and deductive reasoning work together to deliver logical thinking; however, higher thinking demands a grasp of this complex process. Understanding how both forms of reasoning work and their limitations can prevent faulty reasoning. Mistakes in reasoning are called logical fallacies and should be avoided.

Most fallacies are the result of hasty or sweeping generalizations where the conclusion is based on few examples or oversimplified evidence, as in the loud Cubans case. Claiming guilt by association; reasoning that because one thing followed another, the first caused the second; arriving at a conclusion without sufficient quality evidence; or restating the original claim as proof, are more examples of hasty conclusions.

Other fallacies are the result of irrelevant reasoning. These include heaving personal attacks on the individual, not the argument; using the fact that others agree with you as evidence; and manipulating appeals to tradition, fame, or powerful emotions as a primary source of support. Appealing to emotions can be a valid persuasive technique, but the entire argument cannot depend exclusively on feelings. Finally, the either/or fallacy, or false dilemma, presumes that a complex question has only two possible answers. It's never just black or white. I don't have to be against "Obamacare" or be a socialist.

Illogical reasoning undoubtedly appears in our culture, sometimes inadvertently; other times, it is deliberately used to manipulate. You should be aware of how these fallacies work. Look for them in your own writing. Though sometimes effective in manipulating the reader, by using them you risk losing credibility while contributing to misleading disinformation. Aim for logic *and* truth!

GPS Your Way
A Little Research

GPS satellites circle the earth twice a day in a precise orbit and transmit signal information to earth. GPS receivers take this information and use triangulation to calculate the user's exact location.

Too bad we can't use GPS devises to determine our writing topics or locate required information. Instead, we have to do it ourselves as writers.

The word research can be off putting to many students, but research simply means looking for details, information, or direction outside of oneself. For personal essay writing, it can mean looking at family photographs, interviewing relatives, driving to the place being described, discussing other students' experiences, browsing through magazines. In personal essays, you're not necessarily looking for facts or statistics; then again, you are searching for additional details and perspectives related to your topic. Photographs, conversations, personal visits can spark your memory.

Expository writing usually demands more formal research. Once you determine your topic, start by jotting down a series of questions you or your readers may want answered, which may include: What would my target reader most want to know about this topic? What is its most significant element? What do people know least about the topic? What can I contribute to the discussion? Where can I find interesting supporting details and facts? Let such questions guide your explorations.

Most students immediately turn to on-line searches, but don't forget books, library reference sources, or librarians themselves as resources of information for both books and digital materials. On-line research is handy, fast, and abundant; however, make sure you are using academically respectable sources. Inspect the source for reliability, balance, and credibility. It's helpful to understand the purpose of the website. Also make sure the source is current. Try using "Google Scholar" as a starting point since it allows you to search specifically for scholarly literature.

Your school's library website will also offer valuable tools. Take a few minutes to familiarize yourself with it. It will provide access to databases and indexes. Moreover, it may offer links to tutorials and guides to the research process. Most schools also have a Writing Center or Lab to help writing students. Schedule a visit.

Do not become intimidated by the term "research paper." All expository writing that makes references to outside sources needs to provide documentation: parenthetical citations within the text that identify the author's last name and the page number. Additional information on the title, the publisher, and the date and location of publication will be provided at the end of the essay in a "Works Cited" page, both following MLA, or APA, guidelines. Teachers usually review these in class and/or assign textbooks which include them.

If you are not familiar with writing a research essay or MLA or APA guidelines, you have various options: an extensive writing handbook which includes several chapters on research; a specific book just on research strategies; or online free websites such as the one offered by Purdue University: http://owl.english.purdue.edu/owl/resource. This website is an excellent resource for all writing questions, including research.

My students are in the habit of always documenting outside sources, even in journal writing, so the longer essays don't feel so overwhelming. You might want to do the same. Think of the "Research Paper" as simply a longer documented essay. One that demands more proof than your average essay.

The bottom line: Do not be intimidated by the term research and make use of all the resources available to you, online or at your school.

Don't Forget to Breathe
Enjoying the Process

If you've arrived at this chapter after reading all the other ones first, I congratulate you! If you've skipped ahead to the end, turn around. Do yourself a favor. You will not, cannot, succeed at writing, nor enjoy it, without acquiring the tools introduced in earlier sections. They have been included to guide you to this point, where you feel in control of your writing by knowing what to do. Some of the material may have seemed tedious or required multiple readings, so be it. If you find yourself weak in a particular area, review that chapter before every assignment, until it becomes second nature.

Some of my students try so hard to be "good writers" or become so driven by self-criticism that they suffocate their own creative energies. Don't be one of them. Relax, take a deep breath and have fun.

No matter what the writing assignment, by now you can say to yourself: OK, I know how to achieve this. Mind over matter. If you are trying to succeed in a sport, a musical performance, a construction project, or an essay, triumph will come from a combination of knowledge, skill, willingness to do the hard work, and self-assurance. You have educated yourself about the writing process; now practice what you have learned with the confidence that you have the capacity to put on paper what you know.

Slow down; do not rush. Give yourself enough time to linger with your topic, whether a few minutes for an in-class essay or a few hours for a take home assignment. Lingering means giving yourself time to chill and generate ideas. Hopefully, you've experimented with different techniques and found the one that suits you best. If you need to research further, do so without hyperventilating. It's to be expected, so don't fight it. And, of course, leave time to revise, and revise, and revise, especially the home assignments.

Trust the techniques you've learned and trust yourself; it will help you calm down. Being relaxed will make you more creative and effective, which in turn will make you feel satisfied. The more you enjoy, the more energy you'll inject into the piece.

Excellent writing exudes a palpable force which is hard to explain, but easy to feel.

Watching my students develop in-class essays, I always note how the strongest writers give off the most energy. It's like they inhabit an invisible zone. The way they sit, hold their pens, focus down on their papers reveals a powerful connection to the material. This link figures in their success.

If you have ever danced, stretched in a Yoga class, played a sport, you understand what I mean. A huge difference can exist in the way two people hold out their arms, one nonchalantly, another with tension and vitality, as if making a statement with his or her body. That kind of energy is what you need in your writing.

You find it by preparing well and discovering something that matters, to you and to others. In other words, by caring. That's probably the hardest thing to teach. How do you make someone care? Yet this has to happen, regardless of the topic. It's up to you. Find something in each essay to care about.

Caring will imbue your writing, and your life, with the vigor to succeed and especially to enjoy! So get going and type away!

This is an eclectic list of contemporary books my students and I have enjoyed, in no particular order.

Have fun exploring!

(NF Non-fiction F Fiction)

Edwidge Danticat, *Claire of the Sea Light* (F) or
Brother I'm Dying (NF)
Jimmy Santiago Baca, *A Place to Stand* (NF)
Neil Gaiman, *The Ocean at the End of the Lane* (F)
Kevin Powers, *The Yellow Birds* (F)
Susan Caset, *The Wave* (NF)
Nechama Tec, *Defiance* (NF)
Tatiana de Rosnay, *Sarah's Key* (F)
Jon Krakauer, *Into The Wild* (NF)
Haruki Murakami, *After Dark* (F)
Carlos Ruiz Zafón, *The Shadow of the Wind* (F)
Koren Zailckas, *Smashed* (NF)
Khaled Hosseini, *The Kite Runner* (F)
Barack Obama, *Dreams from My Father* (NF)
Michael Lewis, *Moneyball* (F)
Carlos Eire, *Waiting for Snow in Havana* (NF)
Rudolfo Anaya, *Bless Me Ultima* (F)
Maya Angelou, *I Know Why the Caged Bird Sings* (F)
Esmeralda Santiago, *When I Was a Puerto Rican* (NF)
Toni Morrison, *Beloved* or *The Bluest Eye* (F)
Julia Alvarez, *How the Garcia Girls Lost their Accents* (F) or
In the Time of the Butterflies (F)
Ben Joravsky, *Hoop Dreams* (N-F)
Sebastian Junger, *The Perfect Storm* (NF)
Michael Ondaatje, *The English Patient* (F)
Frank McCourt, *Angela's Ashes* (NF)
Bernard Malamud, *The Natural* (F)
Junot Díaz, *The Brief Wondrous Life of Oscar Wao* (F)
Marie Arana, *American Chica* (N-F)
Tea Obreht, *The Tiger's Wife* (F)
Alice Sebold, *Lovely Bones* (F)

Leif Enger, *Peace Like a River* (F)
Aimee Bender, *The Particular Sadness of Lemon Cake* (F)
Amanda Coplin, *The Orchadist* (F)
Karen Russell, *Swamplandia!* (F)
Carl Hiaasan et al, *Naked Came the Manatee* (F)
Oscar Hijuelos, *The Mambo Kings Play Songs of Love* (F)
C.C. Medina, *A Little Love* (F)

About the Author

Carolina Hospital is a poet, essayist, and novelist. She teaches composition and literature at Miami Dade College where she was awarded two Endowed Teaching Chairs. Her most recent publication *The Child of Exile: a Poetry Memoir* was published by Arte Público Press of the University of Houston. Her essays and poems have appeared in numerous national magazines, newspapers, and anthologies, including the *Norton Anthology of Latino Literature*, *Prairie Schooner*, Longman's *Literature: An Introduction to Reading and Writing; The Washington Post*, and *The Miami Herald*. She has published six books including the *Instructor's Guide* for Norton's *New Worlds's of Literature*, the novel *A Little Love*, under the pen name C. C. Medina, and *A Century of Cuban Writers in Florida*, a seminal work for understanding the cultural history of Florida. She also participated with 13 Florida authors such as Carl Hiaasan, James Hall, Dave Barry and Edna Buchanan, in the New York Times' bestseller *Naked Came the Manatee*.

The End

CPSIA information can be obtained
at www.ICGtesting.com
Printed in the USA
LVOW10s0524070217
523432LV00006B/31/P

9 781491 240793